EXPLORE

Savannah 2025

Things to do , Budget friendly Travel Tips, Must-See Destinations, Top Itineraries, Restaurants, Must Visit Destination and Places to Explore in Georgia

Daniel Maureen

TABLE OF CONTENT

TRAVELER'S

not engaged in the rendering of legal, financial, medical or professional advice. The content within this book has been derived from various sources

By reading this document, the reader agrees that under no circumstances is the author responsible for any losses, direct or indirect, that are incurred as a result of the use of this information contained within this book, including, but not limited to, error, omissions, or inaccuracies.

❗ ❗ Surprise ❗ ❗

Dear reader, thank you so much for purchasing my book!
To make this book **(much more!)** affordable, I've created a special gift for you!

You can now have access, for FREE, to the Video version of this book with the coloured images!
Keep in mind that All are originally Coloured when the pdf is obtained .

Go to page 137 and follow the instructions to download the **VIDEO TRAVEL LOG** to have a perfect view towards Your Journey.

I hope you'll enjoy it!

Daniel Maureen
(**NB:**▉ Check Page 137 For Your Video) BONUS ❗

Instructions for using the interactive QR code map

Experience Taiwan with ease! Follow these simple steps to find your way to any attraction:

1 Scan the QR Code: Find the QR code and use your smartphone camera or QR code scanner app to seen it.

2 Tap the link: Once scanned, a notification will appear. Tap on it to apen or search for the location details.

3 Select 'Directions' On the opened web page, tap the "Directions" button to get real-time navigation to the attraction.

4 Start your journey: The map will show the best route from your current location to the attraction. helping you get there without any hassle.

UNFORGETTABLE EXPERIENCE AT SAVANNAH GEORGIA

When I first arrived in Savannah, Georgia, I can still clearly recall how it felt like I had entered a classic Southern tale. I didn't even include it in my first itinerary. A friend casually said, "If you're going through Georgia, you have to stop in Savannah." I had planned to go directly to Charleston for a weekend trip. You've never been anywhere like it.

My curiosity overcame me, and I changed my itinerary. The Spanish moss that hung from the enormous oak trees and swayed softly in the breeze as if inviting me to a hidden, magical realm was the first thing that caught my attention as I passed into Savannah. Even though the air was humid, there was a slight saline wind from the river and the gentle aroma of magnolias. It was the type of setting where time seemed to stop right away.

The well-known **Forsyth Park** was my first destination. While folks relaxed on chairs beneath the trees, I recall standing in front of the famous fountain and watching the water fall in graceful streams. A street entertainer was strumming a gentle melody on his guitar, a couple was enjoying a picnic, and a young girl was running over the grass after bubbles. I had the impression that I had wandered onto a set, but everything was so naturally authentic.

I discovered that each street in the Historic District had a distinct personality as I ventured farther into it. Cobblestone streets meandered between antebellum mansions that were all in excellent condition and had interesting tales to tell. My tiny havens were the squares, those well-known public areas that serve as the focal point of Savannah's distinctive city layout. In **Chippewa Square**, where Forrest Gump used to wait on a bus bench, I sat beneath moss-draped oaks and understood why people fell in love with this city.

Savannah has more than simply its picturesque appearance, though. It has layers; some are haunting, others are lovely, and all are fascinating. Curious yet hesitant, I went on a ghost tour one evening. The guide told us stories of hauntings, tragedies, and the spirits that are said to still haunt the area as we made our way through dark lanes. A shiver that had nothing to do with the weather struck me as I stood outside the Sorrel-Weed House. As the guide put it, "**Savannah never lets its stories go**." Perhaps it was the power of suggestion.

And there was the food after that. The meal, oh. The first bite of shrimp and grits I had at a quaint location hidden away from the main tourist streets is still in my dreams. The grits were silky and buttery, the shrimp was tender, and the spiciness was just right. Later, while enjoying a cone of their renowned Tutti Frutti outside **Leopold's Ice Cream**, I noticed horse-drawn carriages gliding around the street.

But it was the people that really made Savannah what it was. I was met with friendly smiles and sincere interest in my origins and the reason I had come to town everywhere I went. A bartender at a tavern by the river encouraged that I sample a house-made peach cocktail, "because it's the taste of Georgia in a glass," and a shopkeeper in City Market talked to me about local artists.

It seemed like I was saying goodbye to a buddy by the time I left Savannah. I fell in love with the city because of how it made me feel, not only because of its history, architecture, or cuisine. As though I had decelerated, thoroughly explored a location, and engaged with its narratives.

I created this guide to help you enjoy Savannah as much as I did. To stroll along its shady streets, savor its delectable aromas, solve its riddles, and—above all—to experience the same awe that surprised me.

A Closer Exam of Savannah's History

In addition to being among the oldest cities in the **US, Savannah, Georgia**, is also among the best preserved. Savannah, a key port city on the Savannah River, was Georgia's first colonial town and was established in 1733 by **General James Oglethorpe**.

Oglethorpe designed the city with an inventive grid plan that prioritized public areas, such as 24 public squares, 22 of which are still standing today, in order to realize his vision of the city as a center of opportunity. Savannah is among the most walkable cities in the United States thanks to its meticulous layout.

The city has a long history in the United States. Savannah had a significant role in the Revolutionary War, particularly during the Siege of Savannah in 1779, when American and French forces tried to recover the city from British forces. The incident cemented Savannah's significance in the struggle for American freedom, notwithstanding the defeat.

Savannah became one of the busiest ports in the South in the 19th century thanks to its thriving cotton trade. The opulent antebellum houses, cobblestone streets, and iron-clad balconies that embellish the Historic District are testaments to the wealth created during this period. However, the city still recognizes this heritage through sites like the **Owens-Thomas House & Slave Quarters** and the African American Monument along River Street, which were established on the backs of enslaved African Americans.

Another important period in Savannah's history is its involvement in the Civil War. Instead of

razing Savannah like other Southern cities, **General William T. Sherman** decided to preserve its beauty by giving it to **President Abraham Lincoln as a "Christmas gift"** after his tragic March to the Sea in 1864. Because of this choice, a large portion of the city's old architecture was kept intact, enabling tourists to stroll through streets that resemble those from more than a century ago.

Without acknowledging the **Gullah-Geechee** people's influence—descended from enslaved Africans who have preserved a distinctive language, food, and cultural traditions—Savannah's cultural fabric would be incomplete.

This rich legacy is honored by museums such as the Pin Point Heritage Museum, which provides visitors with knowledge about one of the oldest African American civilizations in the United States. Savannah has transformed into a living museum, a place where the past and present come together in the most fascinating manner. You can sense the layers of history that make Savannah genuinely ageless whether you're strolling through the Historic District, going to museums, or just relaxing in one of the city's verdant squares.

1.2 Reasons to Make Savannah Your Next Travel Destination

Savannah is not like other Southern cities. It is a town where every square feels like a scene for a movie, where Spanish moss softly sways from old oak trees, and where you can hardly go far without someone saying "hello." The city is an alluring destination because it skillfully combines friendliness, contemporary inventiveness, and historic charm.

Savannah is calling your name for the following reasons:

- **Marvels of Architecture:**
The Historic District of Savannah is an architectural paradise. For those who enjoy history and architecture, the city is a haven of

Georgian mansions, Gothic cathedrals, and traditional row houses with wrought-iron balconies. Highlights include the magnificent Cathedral of St. John the Baptist, also known as the "Sistine of the South," and the Mercer-Williams House, which gained notoriety from the novel and film Midnight in the Garden of Good and Evil.

• **Walkable Charm**: Savannah is one of the nation's most pedestrian-friendly cities thanks to Oglethorpe's grid pattern. Imagine streets with cobblestones, green areas, fountains, and hidden passageways. The 22 ancient squares, each with its own benches, monuments, and moss-covered live trees, each have a distinct personality.

• **A Foodie's Dream**: Savannah's cuisine combines traditional Southern dishes with cutting-edge culinary techniques. Plates of shrimp and grits, fluffy biscuits with gravy, and crispy fried green tomatoes come to mind, but so do creative delicacies like bourbon-glazed pork belly and pecan-crusted flounder. Enjoy family-style Southern cuisine at Mrs. Wilkes' Dining Room for a genuine experience, or savor the elegant dining scene at The Grey, which is housed in a renovated Greyhound bus terminal.

Known as "**America's Most Haunted City**," Savannah is a popular destination for thrill-seekers and ghost hunters. The city's ghost tours provide engrossing tales of its darker history, regardless of your belief in the paranormal. Visit the infamous Sorrel-Weed House, take part in a ghostly pub crawl, or stroll through the gloomy Bonaventure Cemetery.

• **The Arts and Culture Scene:** The city boasts a flourishing arts culture, largely due to the impact of Savannah College of Art and Design (SCAD). Visit galleries, see movies, or go to the SCAD Museum of Art, which has both modern and antique pieces. Savannah is also home to internationally recognized activities that draw musicians, artists, and filmmakers from all over the world, such as the Savannah Film Festival and the Savannah Music Festival.

- **Riverfront Feelings:** A walk down River Street is a must-do when visiting Savannah. A mix of the old and the new can be found along this cobblestone promenade that runs next to the Savannah River and is lined with stores, eateries, and galleries. Take a riverboat trip for sunset views or get a drink in a to-go cup (yep, Savannah permits open containers in the Historic District) while you see the cargo ships passing by.

- **Unlimited Outdoor Spaces:** Savannah boasts an abundance of green spaces for a metropolis. The largest and most well-known park in the city, Forsyth Park, is a 30-acre haven with lots of picnic areas, shaded strolling trails, and a lovely cast-iron fountain. Seasonal festivals and weekly farmer's markets are also held there. Savannah beckons you to take your time, appreciate the present, and let yourself be enchanted by its ageless appeal. There is always something fresh to see in the city, regardless of how many times you have been there.

Season-by-Season Guide to Savannah's Best Times to Visit

Every season gives Savannah a new vibe, and the city has its own cadence.

Depending on your interests, there is always a good time to come, from the vibrant blooms of spring to the serene alleys adorned with sparkling lights in the winter.

Discover how Savannah changes with the seasons and why you might want to schedule your trip around them.

Savannah in Full Bloom in the Spring (March-May)

- **Why It's the Greatest Time:**

Savannah's springtime feels like the city is putting on its best clothes and waking up from a lengthy nap.

Every park and square appears to be straight out of a postcard as the sweet aroma of azaleas, wisteria, and dogwoods in full bloom fills the air. You can spend the entire day seeing the city without becoming too hot or cold because the temperatures are comfortable between *65°F and 80°F (18°C and 27°C).*

Savannah is at its most colorful during this time, making it the ideal time to stroll through Forsyth Park, where the well-known fountain is surrounded by vivid flowers.

As you wander beneath the moss-covered oaks that create dappled sunlight patterns, the Historic District is particularly enchanting.

- **Events You Can't Miss:**

One of the most varied music festivals in the South is the Savannah Music Festival, which takes place in March and April and features jazz, blues, classical, folk, and even global music. The city's historic venues host performances, giving each performance a unique and intimate vibe.

• **St. Patrick's Day Parade**: One of the nation's largest St. Patrick's Day celebrations takes place in Savannah on **March 17.**

Imagine huge parades, vibrant people, green fountains, Irish dancing, and a lot of joyous celebration. The energy is infectious, and the entire city transforms into a massive party.

- **Travel Advice**: Spring is the busiest time of year, particularly on the weekend of **St. Patrick's Day.** Make reservations for your lodging months in advance if you intend to travel in March, and be prepared for a lively city.

It's well worth the trip, but if you want a more sedate experience, try to visit in **April or early May.**

☀ **June through August:** Warm Days, Chilly Nights

• **What to anticipate:** Savannah experiences hot, muggy summers that frequently reach the 90s°F **(32°C).** However, the city is able to cope with the heat. The majority of activities move to the cooler hours of the day, and life slows down. Late-night strolls, dining by the river, and looking for shady spaces beneath the enormous oak trees are all part of the season.

Savannah's gardens thrive due to the humidity, with vibrant blooms and tropical plants bringing color to every nook and cranny. It's also the ideal time of year to enjoy a riverboat tour along the Savannah River after dusk, get a chilled drink, or sit outside on a terrace.

➤ **Best Experiences:**

📌 **Leopold's Ice Cream**: a Savannah staple since 1919, you can't get through a summer without visiting Leopold's. They have handcrafted varieties that are ideal for cooling off, such as Tutti Frutti and Savannah Socialite, which is a combination of milk chocolate, nuts, and bourbon caramel. You'll have to wait in line, but it's worth it, I promise.

📌 **Ghost Tours in the evening**: Savannah's more enigmatic side comes to life when the sun sets and the city cools. The old cobblestone streets become darker, the shadows grow longer, and the ghost stories start. While taking advantage of the cooler weather, evening excursions are an excellent chance to discover more about Savannah's eerie past.

• **Travel Tip:** Schedule your sightseeing for the early hours of the day or right after the sun sets. Spend that time lounging in a shady park or having a long, leisurely meal indoors because the midday heat can be very oppressive. You'll also need water, so remember to bring it!

🍂 **Fall (September-November): Comfortable & Vibrant**

• **Why It's Excellent:**

Savannah offers the ideal mix in the fall: lower temperatures, fewer visitors, and a city decked out in warm colors. It's the perfect time of year for lengthy walks and outdoor meals because the temperature maintains comfortably between 60°F and *80°F (15°C and 27°C).* In order to create a warm, tranquil atmosphere across the city, the parks and squares exchange the vibrant blossoms of spring for orange, crimson, and gold leaves.

Locals especially love this time of year since events are back and the city feels even friendlier due to the slower pace of the season. With the sky becoming rich tones of pink and orange, fall sunsets over the Savannah River are particularly stunning.

➤ **Highlights of the Season:**

The Savannah Film Festival takes place from late October to early November. This festival, which is hosted by Savannah College of Art and Design **(SCAD)**, attracts well-known Hollywood stars while maintaining an emphasis on indie films. Downtown, you might even run into a star or attend a premiere.

📌 **River Street's Oktoberfest:** This vibrant event offers a taste of Europe to the South with its German beer, bratwurst, live music, and riverside vistas. There will be plenty of delicious cuisine, beer gardens, and fun games.

• **Travel Tip:** Savannah is a gastronomic haven in the fall. Seasonal flavors are emphasized in many local eateries, which provide Georgia pecans, sweet potatoes, and fresh pumpkins. You can try pumpkin-spiced pastries, pecan pie, or even butternut squash soup on a cooler night.

• **Why Go:** Savannah experiences moderate, serene winters with temperatures between 40°F and 65°F (4°C and 18°C). Savannah offers pleasant, fresh air that is ideal for walking tours and relaxing afternoons at neighborhood cafes, while the rest of the country struggles with snow and cold temps. Additionally, the city is at its most festive at this time. The old houses are decked out with wreaths, candles, and festive garlands, and the streets are glistening with sparkling lights. It's the perfect time for a leisurely, crowd-free visit because of the slower pace.

➤ **Holiday Occasions:**

Savannah Holiday Boat Parade: As thousands assemble along River Street to watch, picture boats adorned with vibrant lights glide along the Savannah River. November marks the beginning of the holiday season with this enjoyable, family-friendly event.

📌 **Broughton Street Lights:** With lights, wreaths, and seasonal markets, Broughton Street, one of the city's principal shopping avenues, becomes a jolly paradise. It feels like something from a Christmas movie to stroll along the street while sipping hot cocoa.

- **Travel Tip:** Since winter is Savannah's off-season, there are less visitors and cheaper accommodation rates. This is the ideal time of year if you're searching for a low-cost vacation or just want to see the city without the crowds. Additionally, everything feels even more wonderful because of the Christmas decorations.

> **When Should You Go, Then?**

Enjoy festivals and flowers? For vibrant activities and flowering gardens, visit in the spring.

Want to have some fun late at night and can withstand the heat? Ghost tours and riverfront meals are ideal in the summer.

Prefer cozy surroundings and lower temperatures? With good temperatures and less crowds, fall offers the best of all worlds.

📌 **Seeking tranquility and seasonal joy?** Winter is serene, endearing, and a season of joyous lights. Savannah always has something special in store for you when you visit. The city maintains its ageless charm while adjusting to the changing seasons. Savannah has a way of engrossing you in its narrative, whether you're walking beneath blossoming azaleas or exploring amid sparkling holiday lights.

Historic District Highlights

The city's center is Savannah's Historic District, a well maintained neighborhood where each cobblestone street, iron-wrought balcony, and moss-covered oak tells a tale. This **region, which covers over 2.5 square miles,** is among the biggest National Historic Landmark Districts in the United States. Despite being a living museum, it doesn't feel that way. It is lively and full of life since people live, work, and play here.

Regardless of your interests—history, architecture, or simply strolling through quaint streets—the Historic District has something unique to offer. Here's how you can maximize it.

2.1 Squares and Streets You Must See

General James Oglethorpe created Savannah's 22 public squares as part of the city's grand plan in 1733, and they are among its most recognizable

characteristics. Originally designed as public areas for meetings, marketplaces, and public events, these squares are now serene, shaded areas ideal for relaxing, observing people, or just taking in Savannah's ageless appeal.

Every square has an own personality; some are bustling and vibrant, while others have the feel of secret havens away from the masses.

The Best Squares to Visit

➤ 🌳 Chippewa Square

Fans of Forrest Gump will know this location right away. Here, Forrest waited for his bus while chatting with strangers about his life (and his chocolate box) while perched on that famous bench. The square is still one of the most frequented in the city, despite the fact that the real bench was only a movie set and is now kept in the Savannah History Museum.

📌 **Things to Look for:** The statue of the city's founder, General James Oglethorpe, stands boldly in the center, his sword pointing south, signifying Savannah's resistance to Spanish forces in Florida. The Savannah Theatre, one of the oldest functioning theaters in the United States, is one of the stunning buildings that encircle the plaza.

Travel Tip: One of the greatest places to observe people is here. Enjoy the steady stream of visitors, street entertainers, and locals going about their days while you grab a coffee from a neighboring café.

🌳 **Is Monterey Square Savannah's Most Beautiful Square?** Monterey Square is widely regarded as the most picturesque by both locals and tourists. It's a photographer's paradise with its majestic mansions, verdant gardens, and towering oaks.

📌 **What Makes It Unique**: A monument honoring Polish American Revolutionary War hero Count Casimir Pulaski stands at the center of the area. The Mercer-Williams House on the western edge of Monterey Square, however, is the true star of the square. The home has a sense of mystery and intrigue that was made famous by the book and movie Midnight in the Garden of Good and Evil. Its illustrious (and sometimes scandalous) past can be told to you during a guided tour.

• **Architectural Highlights**: Monterey Square is one of Savannah's most picturesque locations, lined with exquisite specimens of Greek Revival and Italianate architecture.

📌 **Travel Tip:** Go there in the late afternoon when the square is bathed in golden light as the sun peeks through the Spanish moss.

Madison Square

A area Rich in History: Named after President James Madison, this area is surrounded by some of the city's oldest structures while maintaining a serene, contemplative atmosphere.

✔ **What to See:** A statue of Revolutionary War hero Sergeant William Jasper, who lost his life at the Siege of Savannah, is positioned in the center. The **Green-Meldrim House**, a magnificent Gothic Revival palace that was General Sherman's headquarters during the Civil War, is also located on the square.

✔ **Atmosphere**: After a morning of sightseeing, Madison Square is the ideal place to relax because it has a more residential vibe and many of benches shaded by the oaks.

✔ **Travel Tip:** For afternoon tea or a light meal, don't miss the neighboring Gryphon Tea Room, which is located in a former apothecary.

🌳 Forsyth Park (A Must-See, Not a Square)

Forsyth Park is frequently regarded as the crown jewel of the Historic District, despite not being one of Savannah's original squares. One of the city's largest green areas, spanning 30 acres, is a popular meeting place for both residents and visitors.

✔ **The Fountain:** Constructed in 1858, the enormous cast-iron fountain at the park's northern end is its most well-known feature. Often dyed green for St. Patrick's Day festivities, it is one of Savannah's most photographed monuments.

➢ How to Proceed:

Stroll Along the Oak-Lined Paths: The park's main promenade is shaded by enormous oaks covered in Spanish moss, which gives the area a surreal feel.

Check out the weekly Saturday Farmer's Market, which offers live music, locally made crafts, and fresh fruit.

📌 **Unwind:** Find a location on the grass or beneath a shade tree, have a picnic, or just read a book.

🌳 Additional Squares to Consider:

Lafayette Square is well-known for being next to one of Savannah's most notable structures, the Cathedral of St. John the Baptist. The area itself is serene, with benches under oak trees and a lovely fountain in the middle.

Johnson Square, which is close to Bay Street and the riverside, is Savannah's oldest and biggest square. Despite being a busy location, it is rich in history, featuring the Nathanael Greene Monument, which honors a hero of the Revolutionary War.

The Tomochichi Monument, which honors the Yamacraw chief who assisted General Oglethorpe in settling Savannah amicably, is located in Wright Square.

• **Iconic Streets to Stroll**: Jones Street Often regarded as one of America's most picturesque thoroughfares, Jones Street is a serene cobblestone avenue dotted with old brick houses, wrought-iron balconies, and towering trees. It is picture-perfect and transports you back in time.

- *Bull Street*: Connecting many of Savannah's most well-known squares, Bull Street runs north-south through the Historic District. In addition, there are stores, galleries, and many of locations to get a drink or a snack.
- **River Street**: There are restaurants, souvenir shops, and antique shops lining this busy riverfront promenade. It is one of the city's most visited tourist destinations because of its cobblestone lanes, converted cotton warehouses into hip locations, and view of the Savannah River.

2.2 Famous Structures and Landmarks

Savannah's Historic District is a veritable gold mine of architectural styles, encompassing Federal, Georgian, Gothic, and Greek Revival designs. With its well-preserved buildings, old churches, and quaint cobblestone lanes, the neighborhood transports visitors back in time.

Must-See Sites in the Historic District of Savannah

Savannah's Historic District is home to numerous landmarks that tell tales of the city's complicated past in addition to showcasing its stunning architecture. From its religious origins to its involvement in important cultural events, each of these famous sites provides insight into Savannah's past. Here is a more thorough examination of seven must-see sites, complete with pertinent information for a more knowledgeable trip.

- **The St. John the Baptist Cathedral**

222 East Harris Street, Savannah, GA 31401 is the address.

- **French Gothic Revival architecture**

Completed in 1876 (rebuilt following a fire in 1899) Admission is free, while donations are welcome.

➢ Important Information:

The Cathedral is one of the most well-known places of worship in the Southeast and is frequently referred to as the "Sistine of the South."

has 81 stained-glass windows with images of biblical scenes and saints that were imported from Innsbruck, Austria.

One of Savannah's tallest buildings, the twin spires rise to a height of 214 feet.

The cathedral's interior features a pipe organ with more than 2,000 pipes, an elaborate white marble altar brought from Italy, and hand-painted murals.

The church is still in operation, hosting frequent masses and weekly open tours.

📌 **Travel Tip**: Go early in the morning to take in the gentle sunlight that streams through the stained-glass windows, bringing out the rich hues and elaborate patterns.

➤ House of Mercer-Williams

Address: Monterey Square, Savannah, GA 31401, 429 Bull Street Italianate architectural style Year of completion: Construction began in 1860 but was postponed until 1868 because of the Civil War.

• **Admission**: *$12-$15 per person for guided tours*

➤ Important Information:

created for Hugh Mercer, the great-grandfather of musician Johnny Mercer, by architect John S. Norris.

became well-known throughout the world thanks to John Berendt's best-selling novel and movie Midnight in the Garden of Good and Evil, which told the story of Jim Williams, the house's subsequent owner, and his contentious trial.

Original period furnishings, artwork, and personal items from Jim Williams' vast collection may be found throughout the house.

The top levels are still privately held by the Williams family, although the ground floor is accessible to the general public.

boasts a striking mahogany staircase, elaborate crown moldings, and marble mantels.

📌 **Travel Tip:** To completely understand the house's significance in Savannah's cultural past and to gain further perspective, read Midnight in the Garden of Good and Evil before your visit.

The Slave Quarters and the Owens-Thomas House
Address: 124 Abercorn Street, 31401 Savannah, GA
Style of Architecture: English Regency

➤ **Year of Completion: 1819**
The Telfair Museums Pass ($25 for adults and $5 for children) includes admission.

➤ **Important Information:**
The home, which was created by architect William Jay, is regarded as one of the finest specimens of English Regency architecture in the US.
Built for Richard Richardson, a wealthy trader, it was later purchased by George Welshman Owens, whose family occupied it until the early 1900s.
Slave quarters have been kept in one of Savannah's few historic homes, providing a candid and unvarnished glimpse into the lives of the enslaved laborers.

highlights the **Gullah-Geechee** custom of having a "haint blue" roof in the slave quarters to ward off ghosts. The house has early 19th-century features like a rainwater collection cistern and an internal plumbing system.

- **The Old Pink House**
Address: 23 Abercorn Street, 31401 Savannah, GA
Georgian architecture
Completed Year: 1771
Viewing the outside is free, however meal costs vary.

➤ **Important Information:**

James Habersham Jr., a well-known cotton grower and dealer, constructed it.

The house was originally built with red bricks, and over time, the bricks bled through the white stucco, giving it its unique pink coloring.

One of the oldest structures still standing in Savannah and a unique specimen of Georgian architecture in the region.

transformed into a classy eatery and pub that is well-known for its traditional Southern fare, which includes she-crab soup, pecan-crusted chicken, and shrimp and grits.

rumored to be haunted, with many accounts of strange events and ghostly sightings, especially in the tavern in the basement.

📌 **Travel Tip**: Even if you're not eating there, visit the Planters Tavern in the basement for a warm drink by candlelight and maybe even hear the bartender share a ghost story.

Savannah, Georgia 31401, 200 Abercorn Street is the address of Colonial Park Cemetery.
Founded: 1750
Free admission

➤ **Important Information:**

is the last resting place of more than 9,000 individuals, including American Revolutionary War veterans. The location of Button Gwinnett's grave, where he signed the Declaration of Independence

was used as a dueling ground in the 18th and 19th centuries, and marks from misfired bullets may be seen on a number of gravestones.
Union soldiers allegedly changed the dates on certain gravestones during General Sherman's March to the Sea during the Civil War for fun, giving the impression that some individuals had

lived for more than 150 years or had passed away before their time.

The cemetery is frequently included in ghost tours that delve into Savannah's eerie past because of its reputation for paranormal activity.

Other Important Landmarks to See:

The Andrew Low House was the residence of Juliette Gordon Low, the founder of the Girl Scouts of the USA, and the home of Andrew Low, a wealthy cotton manufacturer.

One of the oldest African American Baptist churches in the nation, the First African Baptist Church was founded in 1773 and has an African prayer symbol patterned on its ceiling.

One of the first public art museums in the South, Telfair Academy opened its doors in 1886 and features American and European artwork from the 19th and 20th centuries.

2.3 Walking Tours with Self-Guides

The ease of walking around Savannah is one of its best features. The city encourages you to take your time and explore its old streets, shaded squares, and grid-like structure. You may explore Savannah's history, architecture, and culture in depth with a self-guided walking tour, which also allows for impromptu discoveries, such as a quirky boutique, a secret garden, or a nice café.

This comprehensive guide will help you get the most out of your Savannah Historic District walking tour.

The Traditional Historic District Loop (about two to three hours)

This path provides the ideal fusion of Savannah's recognizable sites, peaceful squares, and quaint streets.

- **Commencement: Forsyth Park**

📍 **Why Begin Here:** One of Savannah's biggest green areas is Forsyth Park, which is also home to the city's most photographed landmark—the cast-iron fountain.

📍 **What to Do:** Spend some time walking along the trails bordered by oak trees in the park.

- Explore the Fragrant Garden, which is fun for everyone but especially for the blind and visually handicapped.
- Visit the Forsyth Farmers' Market on Saturdays to enjoy locally produced honey, fresh veggies, and handcrafted goods.
- **First stop:** Monterey Square, which is around ten minutes' walk north.

Mercer-Williams House is the highlight.

➤ Things to Look for:

The Mercer-Williams House, which was made famous by Midnight in the Garden of Good and Evil, is visible.

- Admire the rich vegetation and Italianate buildings that combine to make this one of Savannah's most charming squares.
- Take a guided tour of the mansion if you have the leisure to do so and discover more about its complicated (and scandalous) past.
- Madison Square is the second stop (5-minute walk northeast).
- The Sergeant William Jasper Monument is a highlight.

✔ **What to See:** Sergeant Jasper, a Revolutionary War hero, is honored by the central monument.

The Green-Meldrim House, a magnificent Gothic-Revival palace that was General Sherman's headquarters during the Civil War, is not to be missed.

Seek out SCAD (Savannah College of Art and Design) buildings in the area; the university has made use of many of Savannah's historic buildings.

Chippewa Square is the third stop (3-minute walk north).

✔ **Highlight:** The Bench Spot of Forrest Gump
Because of its appearance in Forrest Gump, this square is well-known. You may stand where Tom Hanks filmed the famous scene, even though the real bench is now in a museum.
In the center of the area is a statue of General James Oglethorpe, the founder of Savannah.
The historic Savannah Theatre, which opened in 1818 and continues to host shows today, is located nearby.

📌 **Stop 4:** Colonial Park Cemetery, which is five minutes to the east on foot

✔ **Highlight:** The Oldest Cemetery in Savannah
More than 9,000 people are buried in this 1750-founded cemetery, including Revolutionary War heroes like Declaration of Independence signer Button Gwinnett.
Because some gravestones were allegedly destroyed for fun by Union soldiers during the Civil War, look for gravestones with altered dates.
The cemetery is a frequent destination on Savannah's haunted tours because of its **reputation for eerie folklore.**

📌 **Stop 5:** St. John the Baptist Cathedral *(7-minute walk north)*
"Sistine of the South" is the highlight.
Admire this magnificent cathedral's French Gothic style and twin spires.
Step inside to admire hand-painted murals, beautiful stained-glass windows from Austria, and a gigantic pipe organ.
Relax in **Lafayette Square**, a serene area with a center fountain and shaded benches, across the street.

Extra Stops to Make Your Tour Better

Consider including these locations if you have more time or wish to go deeper:
Jones Street is the sixth stop, ten minutes' walk west of the Cathedral.

✔ **Why Visit:** Often considered "the prettiest street in America", Jones Street is dotted with red-brick townhomes, wrought-iron balconies, and giant oak trees. It's a wonderful spot for a leisurely walk and taking pictures.

📌 **The Olde Pink House is the seventh stop (7-minute walk north).**

✔ **Highlight:** Originally built in 1771, this house is one of Savannah's oldest and is now a restaurant serving Southern fare.

The Planters Tavern in the basement is a great place to get a drink and take in the classic Georgian-style architecture, even if you don't have time for a meal.

📍 **River Street is the eighth stop (5-minute walk northeast).**

A busy waterfront avenue dotted with eateries, retail establishments, and former cotton warehouses.

✔ **What to Do:** Peruse neighborhood boutiques and antique shops.

Scoop up a sample of praline from Savannah's Candy Kitchen.

- From the cobblestone promenade, observe the enormous cargo ships as they sail down the Savannah River.

Advice for Self-Guided Walking Tours

Comfortable footwear is essential because Savannah's picturesque cobblestones are uneven and stunning.

1• **Keep hydrated:** Carry a water bottle to stay cool, especially during the warmer months.

If you're fatigued, take use of Savannah's free DOT shuttle, which runs around the Historic District.

2• Give yourself time to explore: Whether it's finding a secret garden, an eccentric bookshop, or a hidden café, some of Savannah's most memorable experiences occur when you venture off the usual route.

4• An Example of a Walking Tour Routes:
A Few Highlights One-hour tour
Begin at Chippewa Square, the location of Forrest Gump.

✔ Proceed to Colonial Park Cemetery, which ends at St. John the Baptist Cathedral.

➢ Advice for Your Own Tour:
1• Put on comfortable shoes: Despite their attractiveness, the cobblestones are harsh on heels and sandals.

2• Drink plenty of water; the humidity can catch you off guard, especially if you're traveling in the spring or summer.

3• Make use of a printed guide or a map app: Even though Savannah is simple to navigate, using a map ensures you don't miss any important locations.

4• Take your time: Savannah's slower tempo adds to its allure. Enjoy the wind among the mossy oaks, people-watch, or just sit in a square.

Top Attractions & Hidden Gems

3.1 The Well-Known Fountain in Forsyth Park

✔ **Address**: Drayton Street and W Gaston Street, Savannah, Georgia 31401
Daily hours: 7 AM to 11 PM

- **Free admission**

📌 **Why It's Iconic:** Forsyth Park serves as the city's common living area in addition to being Savannah's most recognizable green area. Since the **1840s**, this **30-acre** park has served as a meeting spot for both locals and tourists. It's the ideal spot to unwind, explore, or people-watch because it combines nature, history, and culture.

The park's centerpiece is the renowned cast-iron fountain, which was put in place in 1858 and is now one of the most photographed locations in the city. It is renowned for its timeless design, which was influenced by the fountains of Paris' Place de la Concorde. It features graceful tiers, sculpted figures, and water jets that provide a calming background.

A feature of Savannah's well-known festivities, the fountain is given a festive makeover on St. Patrick's Day when the water is dyed vivid green.

➤ Important Points to Examine:
■ **The Forsyth Fountain**

This fountain, which is located at the park's north end, makes for a great photo opportunity. It is encircled by seats, paved paths, and the classic Savannah scenery of tall live oaks covered in Spanish moss.

■ **Fragrant Garden:** Pay attention to the elaborate cast-iron accents and the statues of women holding jugs, which are typical of fountain designs from the 19th century.

The Fragrant Garden, an enclosed sensory experience created especially for the blind but appreciated by everyone, is tucked away in a more sedate area of the park.

It's a tranquil haven away from the more crowded park sections, full of fragrant flora including gardenias, lavender, jasmine, and rosemary.

▪ Farmers' Market on Saturday:

Local farmers and craftspeople erect booths along the park's southern edge every Saturday morning. Fresh food, honey, candles, soaps, and even artwork from the area are all available.

Live music is frequently performed, so you may take in the local cuisine while having fun.

▪ Sports courts and playgrounds:

✔ Suitable for families? Of course. There is a playground in the park featuring swings, slides, and climbing frames for children of various ages. In addition, there are open fields where residents frequently play soccer, frisbee, or even do yoga sessions among the trees, as well as tennis and basketball facilities. Paths for Jogging and

✔ Walking:
Paved walkways run the length of the park, making it ideal for a morning jog or a leisurely stroll. Even in the warmest months, it's pleasant because of the shade provided by the tree-canopied paths.

▓ Memorials for Veterans:

Forsyth Park serves as a place of memory in addition to being a leisure area. A number of war memorials may be found around the central promenade, such as the Confederate Memorial, which was built in 1879 to commemorate Georgian soldiers who lost their lives in the Civil War.

Activities & Events for the Season

🎨 Park Art:

Local artists exhibit and sell their creations under the trees all year long; consider handcrafted jewelry, paintings, and pottery.

🌲 Decorations for the holidays:

The park is adorned with festive displays and sparkling lights during the winter holidays, creating a warm and enchanted atmosphere for visitors to enjoy after dark.

🎵 Concerts outside:

Festivals and outdoor performances are periodically held in Forsyth Park. There's always something going on, from food truck festivals to jazz concerts.

Places Nearby That Are Worth Seeing

1• Forsyth's Collins Quarter:
Coffee and pastries are served at this quaint café with a walk-up window close to the park. Locals adore their Aussie-style brunches and lavender mochas.

2• SCAD Art Museum:
Thanks to the influence of the Savannah College of Art and Design (SCAD), this museum of contemporary art, which is only a short walk from the park, features works by both well-known and emerging artists.

3• Perch:
With a view of the treetops in Forsyth Park, the rooftop bar at the neighboring Local 11ten restaurant serves craft cocktails and small meals.

Fun Facts About Forsyth Park

1• Origins of the Fountain: Despite its distinctive appearance, the fountain is actually a component of a mass-produced design that was available for purchase in a 19th-century catalog. Similar fountains can be seen in Cuzco, Peru, and Poughkeepsie, New York.

2• Haunted Rumors: Some people think the park is haunted, just like many other places in Savannah. Late-night apparitions surrounding the fountain are frequently mentioned on local ghost tours.

3• Film Appearances: "Midnight in the Garden of Good and Evil" is one among the many movies and television series that have starred Forsyth Park, solidifying its reputation as a cultural icon.

📌 The Cemetery of Bonaventure

Location: Thunderbolt, GA 31404, 330 Bonaventure Road 📍 Free admission | ⚫ Hours: 8 a.m. to 5 p.m.

✔ **Why Go**: Bonaventure Cemetery creates a memorable experience by fusing historical history with eerie beauty. The cemetery's popularity goes much beyond its role in Midnight in the Garden of Good and Evil, which made it famous throughout the world. It resembles a landscaped garden rather than a graveyard with its moss-covered oaks, Victorian-era statues, and meandering walkways.

Bonaventure, which is perched on a bluff with a view of the Wilmington River, embodies Savannah's serene, even otherworldly spirit.

✔ **Highlights**: The grave of Gracie Watson: One of the most popular locations, this life-sized statue pays tribute to a young girl who died in 1889 and has become a local legend.

The grave of Johnny Mercer, the renowned songwriter of Moon River, Days of Wine, and Roses, is frequently embellished with mementos from admirers.

✔ **Victorian-Era Statues & Tombstones**: The cemetery is dotted with elaborate ironwork, Gothic-style mausoleums, and elaborate headstones.

✔ **Bonaventure Chapel:** Despite its modest size, this chapel gives the grounds a special, hallowed feel.

• **Travel Tip:** When the sun is shining through the Spanish moss and creating striking shadows, it is best to visit in the late morning or early afternoon.

📌 **Guided Tours:** The cemetery's well-known (and notorious) inhabitants are the subject of entertaining walking tours given by local guides.

3. River Street: Between Montgomery and East Broad Streets, along the Savannah River ▪ Free admission |
● **Hours**: Open around-the-clock (restaurants and stores have different hours).

✔ **Why Go**: A walk down River Street is a must-do when visiting Savannah. This waterfront neighborhood, which was once the epicenter of Savannah's thriving cotton trade, has been turned into a bustling cluster of stores, eateries, and art galleries. It feels antique due to its cobblestone walkways and iron footbridges, but it is kept lively by the energy of street performers and the views of the harbor.

As the sun sets over the river, you can enjoy local delights, buy for unusual presents, and watch enormous cargo ships pass by.

📌 **Highlights**: River Street Sweets is well-known for its freshly made pralines, which you may taste as soon as you enter.
The Olympic Torch Monument was built to commemorate Savannah's hosting of sailing events during the 1996 Olympic Games.

Florence Martus, who waved at ships as they reached the harbor for more than 40 years, is honored by the Waving Girl Statue.

✔ **Dining by the River**: There are many options for dining by the river, ranging from sophisticated riverfront eateries like Vic's on the River to seafood shacks.

✔ The Savannah Belles Ferry is a fun way to view the skyline from the water and offers free rides across the river.

🐾 **Travel Advice**: The best time to go is in the early evening, when the river is illuminated by the golden hour and the street entertainers are at their peak.

✔ **Local's Secret**: For some of Savannah's greatest burgers and a pint, visit The Cotton Exchange Tavern.

✔ **Extra Undiscovered Treasure**: Wormsloe Historic Site
📍 **Address**: 7601 Skidaway Road, Savannah, GA 31406
🎟 **Adult Admission**: $10 |
⚫ 9 a.m. to 5 p.m.

✔ **Why Go:** Wormsloe Historic Site is the ideal location for that classic Savannah snapshot. Its 1.5-mile oak avenue, which is bordered by more than 400 live oaks, forms an incredibly beautiful natural tunnel. Explore the colonial-era ruins, picturesque paths, and a tiny museum showcasing Savannah's early history outside the famous entryway.

There is a lot of open space that is ideal for picnics, so bring a blanket. Enjoy a leisurely afternoon on the grass while grabbing some regional fare from the Farmers' Market or neighboring cafés.

1• **Keep Hydrated**: Bring water, especially during the warmer months, or grab a cold brew or iced coffee at The Collins Quarter.

2• **Plan Around Events**: If you want a more sedate experience, check local event calendars prior to your visit, as large festivals and events can make the park congested.

➤ 3.2 Bonaventure Cemetery
• **Location:** Thunderbolt, GA 31404, 330 Bonaventure Road
- **Hours:** 8 AM to 5 PM, every day

- **Free admission**
  - ## The Reason It's Well-Known:

Bonaventure Cemetery, made famous throughout the world by John Berendt's Midnight in the Garden of Good and Evil, is sometimes referred to as eerily beautiful. It covers more than 100 acres and is perched on a bluff with a view of the Wilmington River.

It is encircled by tall oaks covered in Spanish moss and features sculptures and aged tombstones. Founded in 1846, it serves as an outdoor museum of Savannah's history in addition to being a cemetery.

- ## Bonaventure's highlights include:

The burial of six-year-old Gracie Watson, who died in 1889, is marked by a life-size statue that is one of the cemetery's most frequented locations. Her grave has come to represent mourning and local folklore.

The grave of the renowned songwriter Johnny Mercer, who wrote hits like Moon River and Hooray for Hollywood, is located here. Fans frequently leave letters and tiny mementos on his gravestone.

📌 **Iconic Statues & Ironwork:** Bonaventure is replete with Gothic statues, distinctive tombs, and intricate ironwork that capture Savannah's riches and taste in art in the 19th century.

✔ **Travel Tip:** For more in-depth historical context and engrossing tales about the individuals interred there, schedule a guided Bonaventure Cemetery Tour or take a self-guided tour utilizing a printed map. The ideal lighting conditions for photography are in the early morning or late afternoon.

3.3 Undiscovered Locations Only Locals Are Aware of

Even though Savannah's major attractions are amazing, there are a ton of undiscovered treasures in the city. Here are several local favorites that highlight the more subdued and quirky aspects of the city.

✦ The Market and Brocante in Paris

36 W Broughton St, Savannah, GA 31401 is the address.

French antiques, handcrafted products, and distinctive décor abound in this lovely concept store. For a mid-walk break, the adjoining café

offers some of the best macarons and lavender lattes in the city.

☐ The Factors Walk

✔ **Location**: Between Bay and River Streets, running parallel to River Street a secret system of iron bridges and cobblestone streets that was formerly the center of Savannah's cotton industry. The neighborhood is now calmer and teeming with tiny boutiques, antique stores, and enigmatic doors. It is also said to be among the most haunted places in the city, particularly at night.

➢ How to Proceed:

- Look through shelves filled with jewelry, home décor, and unusual presents.
- Visit the café for freshly baked macarons and a lavender latte.
- No two visits are the same because the store frequently switches up its exhibits.

- **Travel Tip**: You may observe folks on Broughton Street from the café's window seats.

The location of Factors Walk is between Bay Street and River Street

✔ The Reason It's Unique:
Once the epicenter of Savannah's thriving cotton industry, Factors Walk is a truly hidden gem, a labyrinth of cobblestone passageways, iron footbridges, and brick warehouses. The name comes from the fact that cotton brokers, or "factors," operated here in the 19th century.

➤ How to Proceed:

1• Investigate the passageways adorned with enigmatic doors and iron gates.
2• Explore vintage stores or stop by tiny businesses tucked away behind the old buildings.
3• It's ideal for an evening ghost tour because it's one of Savannah's most haunted locations.

✔ Travel Tip: If you want the best light to filter down the little passageways and create the ideal photo opportunity, visit in the late afternoon.

Adult admission to Wormsloe Historic Site is $10. The site is located at 7601 Skidaway Road, Savannah, GA 31406. 9 a.m. to 5 p.m.

➤ The Reason It's Unique:

One of Savannah's most photographed locations is the 1.5-mile boulevard lined with oak trees that leads to Wormsloe.   One of Georgia's first colonists, Noble Jones, lived on the estate, which was built in 1736.   The location offers expansive views of the marsh, picturesque walking routes, and tabby remnants from the colonial era.

> ### How to Proceed:

1• Take breathtaking pictures as you stroll beneath the well-known Oak Avenue.

2• Discover the Tabby Ruins, which are among Georgia's oldest.

3• Learn about Savannah's colonial past by visiting the museum.

> ### District of Starland

Location: south of Forsyth Park, centered on Bull Street

The Starland District, which was formerly a run-down area of the city, is now Savannah's bohemian, artistic district. Today, it's a bustling neighborhood with independent shops, cafés, craft breweries, and murals.

> ## How to Proceed:

1• Get coffee at Foxy Loxy Café, which is well-known for its Tex-Mex brunch and welcoming garden.

2• Take pictures of the area's eccentric art scene as you stroll past vibrant street paintings.

3• Go to Starland Yard, a bustling food truck park including a rooftop bar, live music, and rotating vendors.

- **Travel Tip:** Go during First Friday Art March, when local businesses and galleries open for food, music, and art exhibits.

- **Location:** 109 Martin Luther King Jr. Blvd., Savannah, GA 31401 ✦ The Grey 📍

➤ **The Reason It's Unique:**

Set in a magnificently renovated 1938 Greyhound Bus Terminal, The Grey is more than simply a restaurant; it's a gastronomic experience. James Beard Award-winning chef Mashama Bailey crafts a cuisine that updates classic Southern fare without sacrificing style.

• **Things to Try**: A tasty homage to traditional Southern comfort cuisine is oxtail and grits.
Unique twists on local favorites include smoked collard greens or deviled crab.
Enjoy a specialty cocktail from the retro-style bar to go with your meal.

✨ Local Classic Leopold's Ice Cream

📍 **Address**: 212 E Broughton St, Savannah, GA 31401

Leopold's Ice Cream is a Savannah institution that was established in 1919. The vintage soda fountain offers traditional ice cream tastes created with original formulas. There will likely be a long line, but the wait will be worthwhile.

➤ **What to Purchase:**

A house specialty that has been served since the beginning is the well-known Tutti Frutti.

For a nostalgic treat, try a milkshake or a classic banana split.

Located at 6 E Liberty St., Savannah, GA 31401, The Book Lady Bookstore 📍

Local authors, unique treasures, and new and used books abound at this welcoming independent bookstore. For many years, the Book Lady has been a beloved local hangout for book lovers seeking a peaceful haven.

➤ **How to Proceed:**

1• Look through the historical non-fiction and Southern literature books on the shelf.

2• They frequently have author readings and signings, so check out their event calendar.

3• Sip coffee and read a good book in the back room.

✦ **9924 Pin Point Ave., Savannah, GA 31406 is the address of the Pin Point Heritage Museum.**

The Pin Point Heritage Museum, housed in a former oyster and crab factory, chronicles the history of the Gullah-Geechee people who have inhabited this region for more than a century. The museum showcases the distinctive language, customs, and culture of this African-American group with a long history in Savannah.

➢ **How to Proceed:**

1• Go on a guided tour with locals who will share their cultural perspectives and personal experiences.

2• Discover how to make nets, harvest oysters, and do other traditional crafts.

3• **Travel Tip:** If you're going to Wormsloe Historic Site, the museum is a great place to stop because it's only outside the city.

Culinary Journey Through Savannah

4.1. Classic Southern Cuisine You Can't Miss

Savannah's rich Southern heritage, ethnic variety, and inventive spirit are all reflected in its delectable food scene. The city is well-known for its traditional Southern comfort food, but it also has a fascinating blend of f,arm-to-table restaurants, modern cuisine, and historic restaurants that take you back in time. Savannah offers mouthwatering nibbles wherever you look, whether you're enjoying buttery shrimp and grits, drinking sweet tea on a shady porch, or taking a food tour of the Historic District.

To fully experience the essence of Savannah, this culinary adventure will lead you through the must-try foods, best restaurants, and top food tours.

4.1 Traditional Southern Food You Must Try

For those who enjoy Southern comfort food, Savannah is a haven. These are the foods that characterize the city's culinary profile; they are rooted in tradition but are also amenable to contemporary changes.

- 🥣 **Soup with She-Crab**

What It Is: Blue crab meat, crab roe, heavy cream, and a dash of sherry combine to make this creamy, bisque-like soup. Flavorful, rich, and frequently offered as an appetizer in Savannah's upscale restaurants.

- **Where to Try:**

Their version, The Olde Pink House, is served in a warm, historic atmosphere and is silky and full of fresh crab.

Known for its sophisticated rendition of this traditional soup, Elizabeth on 37th is a fine-dining mainstay in a Southern house.

- **🌿 Greens Collard**

What It Is: A classic Southern side dish, collard greens are slow-cooked with smoked ham hocks, onions, and garlic. It is frequently seasoned with vinegar and a little spicy sauce.

- **Where to Try:**

Mrs. Wilkes' Dining Room: A family-style gathering where cornbread and fried chicken are served with collard greens.

A more sophisticated version of this meal is provided by The Grey, which occasionally twists it by using smoked turkey in place of pork.

🍚 Hoppin' John

What It Is: A classic Lowcountry dish prepared with rice, black-eyed peas, onions, and spiced bacon or ham. Because it is thought to bring good fortune, it is particularly well-liked around New Year's.

- **Where to Try:**

The Grey – Well-known for its sophisticated interpretations of Southern favorites, their Hoppin' John is robust and tasty.

A lighter, more contemporary variant that goes nicely with seasonal salads is the Collins Quarter.

🦀 Crab Cakes

What It Is: Pan-fried to a golden brown using breadcrumbs, seasonings, and sweet blue crab meat. usually served with tartar sauce or remoulade.

- **Where to Try:**

Vic's on the River – Their crab cakes come with a lemon aioli and are stuffed full of crab meat.

Savor fresh crab cakes at The Wyld Dock Bar, which has an outside deck with a view of the marsh.

- **Deviled Eggs**

What It Is: Hard-boiled eggs that have been cut in half and filled with a tangy, creamy yolk mixture; they are frequently garnished with bacon or paprika. An easy yet popular appetizer in the South.

- **Where to Try:**

The Grey – Chef Mashama Bailey uses herbs and pickled shrimp to give it a more upmarket flavor.

Elizabeth on 37th – They use fresh herbs and a little Southern flair in their traditional deviled eggs.

"Cornbread"

What It Is: A traditional Southern dish made with cornmeal that is baked or fried in a skillet until golden. Some varieties, which are frequently served with butter or honey, are sweet, while others are more savory.

- **Where to Try:**

Their family-style dinners were served in Mrs. Wilkes' dining room, warm and buttery.

The Grey Market is a laid-back place that serves cornmeal muffins that go well with fried chicken or collard greens.

🥜 Peanuts boiled

What It Is: These green peanuts, sometimes referred to as the "caviar of the South," are boiled in salted water until they become tender and salty. In Georgia, it's a traditional roadside snack.

Where to Try:

Freshly cooked peanuts are frequently sold in paper bags by local merchants at Savannah's Farmers' Market

The Crab Shack – While you wait for your Lowcountry Boil, grab a basket.

🥒 Butter and Bread Pickles

What It Is: Cucumber slices pickled in a sweet and tangy brine, frequently used as a sandwich topping or side.

Where to Try:

The bakery Back in the Day is well-known for using these pickles into their well-known sandwiches.

The Grey Market – Sells butter pickles and jars of homemade bread.

➤ Pie with Sweet Potatoes

What It Is: A traditional Southern dessert consisting of sugar, spices, mashed sweet potatoes, and a flaky crust. It's a creamy, sweet substitute for pumpkin pie.

- **Where to Try:**

The traditional sweet potato pie with fresh whipped cream on top is the specialty of Back in the Day Bakery.

Sweet potato pie is occasionally offered as a seasonal flavor at Leopold's Ice Cream.

4.2 Top Cafes, Restaurants, and Dining Establishments

Savannah's food culture is diverse, ranging from fancy restaurants to oddball cafés and laid-back dives. Locals adore these locations, and tourists can't stop raving about them:

➤ Famous & Exquisite Dining:

The Grey 🏆

Martin Luther King Jr. Blvd., 109

Feeling: elegant modernism with a touch of the past

Why Go: Under the direction of James Beard Award-winning Chef Mashama Bailey, The Grey, which is housed in a refurbished 1938 Greyhound bus terminal, has won praise from all around the country. Southern classics are reimagined with a cosmopolitan twist on the menu.
Deviled crab, smoked collard greens, and oxtail and grits are must-try dishes.

• **Pro Tip:** For a more relaxed experience, visit the restaurant's Diner Bar, which serves specialty drinks and a simplified menu.

➢ The Pink House of Old
🍀 23 Abercorn Street
Classic Southern friendliness combined with historic charm
This Savannah landmark, housed in an 18th-century estate, serves upmarket takes on Southern favorites in a romantic, lighted atmosphere. Some people even claim it is haunted!
• **Must-Try:** the renowned crispy fried chicken, shrimp and grits, and she-crab soup.

• **Pro Tip:** For a more intimate, speakeasy atmosphere with live piano music, go downstairs to the Planters Tavern.

Elizabeth on the 37th Street, 105 E

The atmosphere of a classic Southern house with exquisite food

The upmarket farm-to-table menu at this quaint, white-columned home features Lowcountry foods and seafood from the area.

Georgia's pecan pie, crab-stuffed fish, and shrimp and grits are must-trys.

• **Pro Tip:** For a romantic meal, request a table next to the windows overlooking the garden.

🫐 Local & Farm-to-Table Favorites

1• Rye & Cotton 🐓

📍 Habersham Street, 1801

Housed in a former bank, the space has a modern yet rustic vibe. House-made breads, charcuterie, and small plates with strong tastes are served at this restaurant, which is well-known for its Southern-inspired, seasonally-inspired meals.

The **house charcuterie board**, pimento cheese toast, and fried chicken wings with pickled celery are must-trys.

- **Pro Tip:** Their Southern Old Fashioned is very good, so don't miss the cocktails.

➤ Savannah, husk 🌿

📍 Oglethorpe Avenue 12 W

Southern sophistication with an emphasis on locally sourced foods

This Savannah location, which is a sibling to the renowned Husk Charleston, serves reimagined Southern cuisine that is exclusively sourced from the Southeast.

- **Heritage pork chops**, the country ham sampler plate, and smoked catfish dip are must-trys.

- **Pro Tip:** There's always something fresh to try because their seasonal menus vary often.

➤ Wyld Dock Bar 🌊

📍 **Livingston Avenue, 2740**

informal dinner by the water with views of the marshes

This place serves fresh seafood and beverages while overlooking the sunset from a serene dock near the marshes.

The shrimp tacos, crab cakes, and lowcountry boil are must-trys.

- **Pro Tip:** For the greatest vistas and a laid-back, beachy atmosphere, get there before sunset.

🍩 Comfortable Cafés & Brunch Locations:

The Quarter for Collins 🍖

151 Bull St.

a café with a Southern flair and Australian influences

The Collins Quarter, which is well-known for its brunch scene, provides a relaxed café experience with strong tastes and creative lattes.

Swine Time Beni (pulled pork eggs benedict), avocado toast, and the spiced lavender mocha are all must-trys.

Pro Tip: For outside eating overlooking the famous fountain, visit their site in Forsyth Park.

• Foxy Loxy Café

Bull Street, 1919

diverse, artistic, and comfortable courtyard atmosphere Foxy Loxy, a Starland District favorite, serves craft coffee, live music evenings, and breakfast with a Tex-Mex flair.

A slice of their pecan pie, a cortado, and tacos with chorizo and egg are must-trys.

Pro Tip: Enjoy wine and live music by the courtyard fire on Fireside Fridays.

The Perceptive Bean ☕

📍 13 E Park Ave

Earthy, artistic, and community-focused vibe

A welcoming café that is ideal for vegetarians, vegans, and coffee lovers, located near to Forsyth Park. With poetry evenings and independent film screenings, it serves as a community hub.

Must-Try: house-made granola, cold brew, and vegan breakfast burrito.

➢ The Ice Cream of Leopold ♣
📍 Broughton Street, 212 E
vintage 1950s soda fountain
Leopold's, a Savannah mainstay since 1919, is renowned for its classic flavors and vintage charm. There will be a queue, but the wait will be worthwhile!

Must-Try: their traditional banana split, honey almond & cream, and tutti frutti

Pro Tip: To avoid huge lineups, go in the middle of the afternoon, which is off-peak.

➢ Bakery Back in the Day
📍 Bull Street 2403
Cozy, old-fashioned bakery
Why Go: Known for its traditional Southern sweets and quaint ambiance, this bakery has been featured on several cooking shows.

Must-Try: Their award-winning cupcakes, banana pudding, and buttermilk biscuits.

Pro Tip: To make these delicacies at home, get a cookbook that has been signed by the proprietors.

Sweets from River Street

📍 13 E River St

Traditional confectionery with a touch of the South

Why Go: Famous for freshly crafted pralines, hand-stretched taffy, and gourmet chocolates. The smell alone will entice you in.

Caramel apples, saltwater taffy, and pecan pralines are must-trys.

Favorites for Nightlife & Bars

1• Alley Cat Lounge

• W Broughton Lane, 207

The atmosphere of a speakeasy-style cocktail bar

• **Why Go:** Well-known for its wide selection of cocktails, which are served in a warm, dimly lit setting. They even include a complete newspaper with their drink menu!

Sazerac, Bee's Knees, and their seasonal cocktail rotation are must-trys.

2• Bar of Artillery
📍 Bull Street 307

The vibe is upscale and has a military theme from the past.

• **Why Go:** This stylish cocktail bar, housed in a former armory, is ideal for a night out.

• Elderflower Collins and the Hemingway Daiquiri are must-try drinks.

3• The Rooftop Bar at Peregrin
📍 256 E. Perry St.

Stylish rooftop with expansive views

• **Why Go:** This rooftop bar provides handmade cocktails and a chic, laid-back atmosphere while overlooking the Historic District.

• **Must-Try:** frosé and Peregrin Punch served with little dishes like truffle fries.

4.3 Savannah's Well-Known Tastings & Food Tours

A cuisine tour is the best way for foodies to taste Savannah's flavors in depth. These trips offer the right blend of history, culture, and, of course, excellent meals.

➤ **Famous Savannah Food Tours:**

Savannah Taste Experience – First Squares Food Tour

Commencing Location: Johnson Square
Time: about three hours
Cost: around $65 per person

➤ **The Reason It's Unique:**

Savannah's historic squares and famous restaurants are combined in this award-winning walking tour. While learning about the city's colonial background and its rich culinary scene, you will visit six local eateries and specialty shops.

📌 **Highlights:**
- Try the freshly prepared pralines, pulled pork sliders, and shrimp and grits.
- For a honey sampling, stop by neighborhood favorites like Savannah Bee Company and Zunzi's, which serve sandwiches with South African influences.
- Finish on a high note with a sweet treat at Wright Square Café.

Pro Tip: There's plenty of food to go around, so arrive hungry and wear comfortable shoes!

Savannah Walking Tour with Southern Flavours

1• **Beginning Location:** Ellis Square
Time: about three hours
Cost: about $60 per person

➤ **The Reason It's Unique:**
While incorporating the city's rich history, this trip concentrates on traditional Southern cuisine. For first-time guests who wish to experience authentic Lowcountry cuisine while learning about Savannah's history, it's ideal.

📌 **Highlights:**
1• Savor sweet Southern iced tea, pimento cheese, and fried green tomatoes.
2• Along the way, try some locally made craft beverages.
3• The Ordinary Pub and The Little Crown by Pie Society, which serves Southern pies with British influences, are frequent stops.

📌 **Pro Tip:** This trip is perfect for foodies who enjoy a good drink with their meal because it includes a stop for a beverage.

2• Amazing Culinary Adventure: Off the Typical Route
Starland District is the starting point.
Time: about three hours
Cost: around $70 per person
   ➤ **The Reason It's Unique:**
Explore the trendy Starland District outside of the Historic District, where unique eats and contemporary restaurants are the highlight. This trip focuses on Savannah's modern food scene.

📌 **Highlights:**
1• Enjoy locally made beer, craft coffee, and artisan pizzas.
2• See locations with live music and rotating food trucks, such as Starland Yard and Foxy Loxy Café.
3• Discover how the area went from being ignored to becoming amazing.

📌 **Pro Tip:** For recurring tourists who want to see more than the usual tourist attractions, this is an excellent tour.
   ➤ **Specialty Tours & Tastings:**
A honey tasting bar run by Savannah Bee Company
104 West Broughton Street
Available for walk-in tastings | **$ Cost:** $15 for mead flights, free tastings

This isn't just any honey store. You can taste both domestic and foreign honeys at Savannah Bee Company, including the uncommon Tupelo honey and wildflower honey. Enjoy honey wine, an old beverage that is having a modern resurgence, at their mead tasting bar.

➤ **Must-Try:**
1• A favorite that is smooth and creamy is Tupelo Honey.
2• Orange Blossom Honey
3• Mead Flight: A selection of sweet, semi-sweet, and dry types

📌 **Pro Tip:** For a distinctive Savannah memento, get a jar of honey (or two).

3• Spirits Tour & Tasting at Ghost Coast Distillery 🥃

641 Indian St.
Daily tours | $ **Cost:** around $12 per person
➤ **What's Different:**
With their craft spirits, Ghost Coast, Savannah's first authorized distillery since Prohibition, is causing a stir. The tour highlights the production of their small-batch spirits while delving into

Savannah's drunken past, including stories from Prohibition.

- **Must-Try:**

1• Tastings of vodka, whiskey, and bourbon liqueurs with unusual flavors, such as lemon and honey and tangerine

2• Their tasting bar's signature cocktails

📌 **Pro Tip:** Sample their Chatham Artillery Punch, a strong, regional libation that dates back to the nineteenth century.

3• Coffee Tasting Experience at Savannah Coffee Roasters ☕

📍 **Liberty Street, 215 W**

Weekend classes are offered | 💲 Cost: about $30 per person

➤ **What's Different:**

Savannah Coffee Roasters, which has been in business since 1909, provides an immersive experience of the coffee roasting process. After learning how they source their beans and perfect their roasts, you'll get to sample their unique mixes and single-origin coffees.

➤ **Must-Try:**

Cold Brew Flight including 3 different sources
Espresso tasting and freshly baked pastries

- Bring a bag of their famous Savannah Blend home with you.

📌 **Pro Tip:** To master the skill of making the ideal latte, enroll in their Barista Class.

4. **Adam Turoni's Chocolate**: The *Chocolate Tasting Experience* 🍫

📍 **Broughton Street, 323 W**

Welcome walk-ins | 💲 Cost: around $20 per person

➢ **What's Different:**

Enter Chocolat by Adam Turoni, a chocolate lover's paradise, which is fashioned after a Victorian library and has bookshelves brimming with chocolate bars and truffles handcrafted by hand.

➢ **Must-Try:**
- Savannah Honey Truffle
- Caramel Bonbons with Salt
- Chocolate Bar with Bourbon and Pecans

📌 **Pro Tip:** Reserve their Chocolate Tasting Experience to enjoy a wine or coffee-paired guided tasting of their finest creations.

Progressive Food Tours for Dinner and Evening

📌 **Walking Tour of Savannah's Cuisine and Culture**

Commencing Location: Johnson Square

⬤ **Cost**: about $70 per person; duration: about three hours

➤ **The Reason It's Unique:**

This evening tour showcases Savannah's diverse cultural influences through a well planned dining experience, making it ideal for foodies who want a little history with their dinner

📌 **Highlights:**

- Serve hors d'oeuvres and a craft cocktail first.
- Go on to robust Lowcountry fare like gumbo and crab cakes.
- Enjoy dessert and a nightcap at one of Savannah's iconic pubs to cap off the evening.

Pro Tip: Since the tour occurs in the evening, it goes well with a stroll through the Historic District at sunset.

📌 **Travel Tip:** Reservations are strongly advised for popular restaurants like The Grey or The Olde Pink House, as many of Savannah's best restaurants fill up quickly. Remember to save space for dessert—the line is worth it for Leopold's Ice Cream!

Savannah's Art, Culture, and Music Scene

5.1. Exploring Local Art Galleries and SCAD

Savannah's rich history is matched by the strength of its artistic and cultural pulse. With its stately antebellum buildings, moss-draped oaks, and cobblestone walkways, the city itself resembles a living artwork.

Beneath that timeless Southern beauty, however, is a thriving, dynamic art community that is driven by creativity, invention, and a strong sense of cultural heritage. Savannah provides a varied fusion of heritage and contemporary culture, whether you're visiting one of the city's well-known festivals, strolling through SCAD's state-of-the-art galleries, or seeing live jazz in a secret club.

Must-See Creative Spaces & Art Galleries

➤ SCAD Art Museum 🏛

Admission: around $10. Hours: Tuesday through Saturday 10 AM to 5 PM, Sunday 12 PM to 5 PM. 📍 601 Turner Blvd.

- **Reasons to Go:**

A mainstay of Savannah's modern art scene, the SCAD Museum of Art is housed in a magnificently renovated railway terminal from the 1850s. In addition to showcasing the artwork of SCAD students and alumni, it features revolving exhibitions by international artists.

- **Things to Look for:**

A vibrant fusion of mixed media, fashion, photography, and sculpture. Huge sculptures and installations can be found in the museum's outdoor Jenkins Courtyard.

Panel discussions, movie screenings, and artist presentations are all part of the regular programming.

The **Walter O. Evans Center** for African American Studies, which features significant pieces by African American artists, is a must-see.

➢ The Gutstein Gallery

201 E Broughton St | ⏰ Open Monday through Saturday from 10 AM to 6 PM | Free Admission

- **Reasons to Go:**

Gutstein Gallery is a sleek, contemporary venue run by SCAD that specializes in presenting avant-garde pieces by both up-and-coming and well-established artists. Anticipate exhibitions that are daring and experimental, pushing the limits of conventional art forms.

- **Things to Look for:**

- **rotating displays by visiting artists, SCAD alumni**, and students.

- regular interactive displays and multimedia projects.

- seasonal pop-up exhibitions that showcase the newest styles in design and art.

 Pro Tip: Visit on the second Saturday of every month for Savannah's Art Walk to meet featured artists and take advantage of complimentary wine tastings.

- **Museums in Telfair** ✏️

Access: ~$25 (covers all three venues) 📍 121 Barnard St | ⏰ Hours: Mon-Sat 10 AM-5 PM, Sun 12 PM-5 PM

- **Reasons to Go:**

 The Telfair Museums, one of the oldest public art museums in the South, provide a diverse collection of modern art, architectural history, and historic art at three different locations:

📌 **Telfair Academy (1812):** This venue, which is housed in a historic mansion, showcases European and American art from the 19th century, including pieces by Childe Hassam and Gari Melchers.

The Jepson Center is a contemporary glass-walled structure that features interactive exhibits, family-friendly events, and contemporary art. The Kahlil Gibran Collection is not to be missed.

A thorough exploration of Savannah's complicated past and Regency-era architecture, including the well-preserved slave quarters that provide a sobering glimpse into the city's past, is provided at Owens-Thomas House & Slave Quarters.

➢ **ShopSCAD** 🌐

Hours: Mon–Sat 10 AM–6 PM, Sun 12 PM–5 PM | 340 Bull St | ⏰ Free Admission

- **Reasons to Go:**

You can buy original artwork created by SCAD instructors, alumni, and students at ShopSCAD, a hybrid art gallery and store. It's the ideal place to get a unique present or keepsake.

- **What to Look for:**

Handcrafted fabrics, ceramics, and jewelry.

Photographs, paintings, and prints by emerging artists.

Fashion items and accessories made by design students at SCAD.

📌 **Pro Tip:** Keep an eye out for special exhibits and artist trunk shows that showcase SCAD's best talent during certain seasons.

➢ **Roots Up Gallery**

📍 6 E Liberty St | ⏰ Open Tuesday through Saturday from 11 AM to 5 PM | Free Admission

Reasons to Go:

Roots Up Gallery features unvarnished, heartfelt pieces that emphasize the distinctive culture and storytelling customs of the South, with a focus on Southern folk art and self-taught artists.

● **Things to Look for:**

vibrant folk paintings and sculptures made of various media.

external artwork created by local and national artists.

Handmade items that capture the essence of Southern culture.

📌 **Pro Tip: Keep** an eye on their calendar for forthcoming events, since this gallery frequently hosts live painting demos and artist presentations.

🎨 **Savannah's Public Art and Murals:**

The city is dotted with sculptures, street art, and vibrant murals that demonstrate Savannah's creative energy. SCAD students are responsible for many of these pieces, which add to the city's live art culture.

➤ **District of Starland** ✏️

Located south of Forsyth Park, centered on Bull Street

● **Reasons to Go:**

The Starland District, Savannah's creative center, is teeming with colorful murals, graffiti, and oddball public sculptures. This neighborhood combines cuisine, music, and art into a single, lively area.

Things to Look for: vibrant murals on the walls of breweries, stores, and cafés.

🎨 Annual Art Celebrations & SCAD Events:

- **April's SCAD Sidewalk Arts Festival**

Every spring, SCAD students and alumni use chalk alone to create vibrant works of art on the sidewalks of Forsyth Park. With live music, food vendors, and lots of photo opportunities, it's one of Savannah's most well-liked art festivals.

The second Saturday of every month is Savannah Art Walk.

a monthly occasion when nearby galleries host free wine tastings, artist meet-and-greets, and special exhibits.

Film Festival at SCAD Savannah (Late October to Early November)

With screenings, panels, and celebrity appearances, this is one of the biggest university-run film festivals in the United States.

5.2 Jazz clubs and live music venues The city's rich, multi-layered soundtrack is produced by Savannah's diverse music scene, which combines folk traditions, indie rock, soulful jazz, and Southern blues. Savannah provides a range of locations where you may see live performances almost every night of the week, from renowned dive bars to sophisticated jazz lounges. Regardless of your preference for a relaxed acoustic performance, an intense rock show, or the mellow tones of a jazz quartet, the city has something to offer.

Top Locations for Live Music

1• Soon to Reopen: The Jinx 🎸

📍 200 W Congress St | ⏰ Dependent on the performance

- Reopening with the same gritty atmosphere and eclectic events, The Jinx is a legendary dive bar that became the center of Savannah's underground music scene for more than 20 years. The Jinx is a popular destination for locals seeking a genuine, unpretentious musical experience because of its small stage, energetic attendance, and laid-back atmosphere.

- **What to anticipate:**

Punk, indie rock, metal, and alternative are among the genres.

It has a vintage dive-bar vibe thanks to the band posters and graffiti art that cover the walls.

Late-night performances frequently develop into wild dance parties.

📌 **Pro Tip:** To find out when they reopen and what shows are coming up, follow them on social media.

2• Plant Riverside's District Live 🎤

Weekly shows at 400 W River St. | ⏰ Ticket prices vary

District Live, located in the exclusive Plant Riverside District, is one of Savannah's newest and most cutting-edge music venues.   With its cutting-edge acoustics and spectacular lighting, the facility is ideal for both local and national touring performers.

- **What to anticipate:**

1• variety of styles, including pop, country, R&B, and rock.

2• VIP seats and views from the balcony for a more luxurious musical experience.

3• Easy access to the many bars, restaurants, and rooftop lounges at Plant Riverside for beverages before or after the show.

📌 **Pro Tip:** Look for pre-show eating packages and happy hour promotions on their website.

3• North Savannah, victory 🎶

Tickets range from $25 to $50. 📍 2603 Whitaker St | ⏰ Depending on the event

- ➤ **Why Travel?**

Victory North is a multipurpose facility with high ceilings, brick walls, and an industrial-chic design, situated in a wonderfully renovated warehouse in the Starland District. It is now a popular location for private gatherings and medium-sized performances.

- • **What to anticipate:**
- a varied lineup featuring musicians from hip-hop, jazz, folk, and indie rock.
- stages for seasonal performances both indoors and outside.
- Pop-up food vendors and a full-service bar are common at larger events.

📌 **Pro Tip:** Depending on the evening, the venue changes because they also organize private events and wedding receptions.

4• The Haunting of The Davenport House

- **Location:** 324 E State St

The Isaiah Davenport House, completed in 1820, is a spectacular example of Federal-style architecture and played a vital part in Savannah's historic preservation effort.   But like many historic mansions in the city, it's not without its ghost legends.

Staff and guests have reported views of a young girl on the higher floors, presumed to be one of the Davenport children who perished in the home. Others have noticed a dark masculine figure, perhaps Isaiah Davenport himself, gazing over the house.   Visitors often tell about frigid areas, doors that open on their own, and even the smell of lavender perfume floating across deserted rooms.

The house offers haunted tours during Halloween, where interpreters narrate eerie tales and encourage visitors to look out for spirit guests.

⚡ Final Thoughts on Savannah's Spooky Legends

Savannah is a location where the past remains, not just in its architecture and cobblestone streets but in the whispers and legends passed down through generations.

Whether you believe in ghosts or simply appreciate a good narrative, the legends of curses, restless spirits, and unsolved riddles give Savannah its haunting enchantment. Goods

Shopping, Markets, and Local Finds

7.1. Boutique Shops and Antique Stores

Savannah is a shopper's paradise in addition to being known for its charming squares and ghost legends. There is something for every taste and price range in the city, from quirky boutiques and artisanal markets to antique stores and locally made goods. Savannah's shopping culture will not let you down, whether you're looking for a unique memento, handcrafted jewelry, or a rare antique treasure.

This is your all-inclusive guide to Savannah's best markets, boutiques, and retail districts, along with addresses and typical prices.

7.1 Antique Stores and Boutiques

Savannah's unique boutiques and antique stores, where you may browse everything from old furniture to handcrafted crafts, are another example of its historic appeal.

🛍 Additional Antique Stores and Boutiques in Savannah

Here are further boutiques, antique shops, and local gems where you can find unique items, ranging from artisan-made goods to rare antiques and stylish clothing, if you want to delve deeper into Savannah's vibrant shopping culture.

Bookseller E. Shaver, 326 Bull St., Savannah, GA 31401

🔔 Sun: 12 PM to 5 PM; Mon–Sat: 10 AM to 6 PM

$ $10 to $50 is the average price range.

- **Why Travel?**

E. Shaver, a charming neighborhood bookshop close to Madison Square, is a true Savannah mainstay. It's a book lover's paradise, complete with creaking wooden floorboards, book-filled nooks, and even store cats relaxing.

Top Discoveries: An extensive compilation of Savannah ghost stories and local history

- Copies of books signed by local writers
- Unique gifts such as tote bags, stationery, and reading mugs

📌 **Pro Tip**: Order a cup and peruse your new discoveries in peace as the store is adjacent to a tea parlor.

- **Savannah, GA 31401**

🏺 Picker Joe's Antique Mall & Vintage Market 🏺

📍 217 E 41st St

Sun: 12 PM to 5 PM | Mon-Sat: 10 AM to 6 PM

💲 $5 to $500 is the average price range.

With more than 10,000 square feet of treasures, Picker Joe's is a haven for vintage enthusiasts and antique hunters. Imagine vintage signs, retro furniture, and oddball trinkets—you could spend hours exploring this kind of place.

➤ Top Discoveries:

1• Typewriters, vintage furniture, and retro décor
  Rare items, old cameras, and records
2• Mason jars and Coca-Cola advertisements are examples of Southern antiques.

📌 **Pro Tip**: For a more sedate shopping experience, go during the week; weekends can be crowded with treasure seekers.

Savannah, GA 31401

🔔 The Book Lady Bookstore 📚

📍 6 E Liberty St   Sun: 11 AM-4 PM | Mon-Sat: 10 AM-6 PM

💲 **$5 to $60 is the average price range.**

With an excellent selection of new, old, and rare books, The Book Lady has been one of Savannah's favorite independent bookstores since 1978. It's a true hidden gem for book lovers with its winding roads and welcoming demeanor.

➤ **Top Discoveries:**

1• First editions that are rare and signed
2• Books and poetry collections of local interest
  Funny stationery and bookmarks

📌 **Pro Tip:** Seek advice from the staff; they are frequently happy to help you find a hidden gem or the writing of a local author.

Old Maps & Prints by V&J Duncan 🗺️

📍 14 W Hull St, Savannah, GA 31401 🔔 Monday through Saturday: 11 AM to 5 PM 💲 Average Cost: Between $50 and $3,000.

Why Go: Visit V&J Duncan, which has a sizable collection of 17th-century maps, prints, and artwork, for a genuinely one-of-a-kind memento.

➤ Top Discoveries:

1• Original Civil War prints and historical papers, as well as old maps of Georgia, Savannah, and the American South

2• Antique zoological and botanical drawings

📌 **Pro Tip**: Looking over maps from centuries ago is like traveling back in time, even if you decide not to purchase.

Savannah, GA 31401 Red Clover Boutique

📍 244 Bull St

🔔 Sun: 12 PM to 5 PM; Mon–Sat: 10 AM to 6 PM

💲 Average Cost: $25 to $150

Red Clover is a must-see for stylish, bohemian clothing. This business is well-known for its reasonably priced, carefully chosen selection of apparel, accessories, and jewelry. It's a great place to find a lovely item to wear while in Savannah.

➤ Top Discoveries:

Flowy jumpsuits and dresses

Handcrafted jewelry and simple accessories

Cozy sweaters, backpacks, and seasonal caps

📌 **Pro Tip**: If you like something, get it before it's gone because they get new items every week!

401 Whitaker St., Savannah, GA 31401 🔔 One Fish Two Fish 📕 📍 Sun: 12 PM to 5 PM; Mon-Sat: 10 AM to 6 PM

💲 Average Cost: $15 to $250

➢ Why Travel?

One Fish Two Fish, a local favorite, provides a thoughtfully chosen assortment of gifts, jewelry, and home décor. The store is great for finding housewarming presents or unusual souvenirs, and it has a Southern-chic atmosphere.

• Top Discoveries:

- Home fragrances and artisan candles
- Serving platters and décor with a coastal theme
- Chic accessories such as scarves and clutches

📌 **Pro Tip:** For more boutique apparel and home décor nearby, check out their sister companies, The Annex and The Annex 2.

Forsyth 106 W Hall St, Savannah, GA 31401 🔔 The Future 🌿

📍 Sun: 12 PM to 5 PM; Mon-Sat: 11 AM to 6 PM
💲 Average Cost: $15 to $250

Why Travel?

The Future on Forsyth is the place to go for those interested in metaphysics and spirituality. It is a delightful boutique that is well-known for its crystals, tarot decks, and mystical delights.

> ➤ **Top Discoveries:**

Spice blends unique to Savannah, such as "Savannah Summer" rub

DIY spice kits and cookery combinations, as well as loose-leaf teas including Peach Apricot and Savannah Chai

📌 **Pro Tip:** Take advantage of their sample jars so you can smell each combination before making a purchase!

7.2 River Street Shopping and the City Market

The commercial environment of Savannah is centered on River Street and the City Market. Both are brimming with Southern charm, handmade products, and local artwork. These ancient retail districts provide an incredible experience, whether you're looking for unique mementos or artisan goods or just want to take in the lively atmosphere.

219 W Bryan St, Savannah, GA 31401 🐚 City Market 📍 Sun: 12 PM to 5 PM; Mon–Sat: 10 AM to 6 PM

💲 Average Cost: $10 to $100

City Market, **which** dates back to the 1700s, has been the center of Savannah's commerce and culture for than 200 years. It is still a thriving outdoor market today, with local shops, art galleries, handcrafted goods, and live music. It's the ideal fusion of entertainment, commerce, and history.

Top Picks in the City Market

1• Art Gallery by A.T. Hun

What You'll Discover: One-of-a-kind sculptures, vibrant contemporary paintings, and hand-blown glass art.

The Reason It's Unique: Bold and whimsical works by regional and international artists are the main emphasis of this collection.

2• Savannah Bee Enterprise

What You'll Find: Mead (honey wine), honey-infused skincare products, and honey produced locally.

The Reason It's Unique: Enjoy sampling at their in-store honey bar and try out unique varieties like Tupelo honey.

3• The Byrd Cookie Company

Southern treats, such as their renowned Key Lime Coolers and Cheddar Pecan Biscuits, are available.

➢ **The Reason It's Unique:**

Ideal for foodies who want to bring a little bit of Savannah home with them.

7.3 Best Souvenirs and Locally Made Goods

Without bringing a little bit of Savannah's charm home with you, your trip wouldn't be complete. Savannah provides a wide range of souvenirs that go beyond standard postcards and magnets, from locally inspired artwork to artisanal treats and handcrafted goods.   These are the greatest locations to find one-of-a-kind, locally produced treasures, whether you're shopping for yourself, friends, or family.

104 W Broughton St, Savannah, GA 31401 ⚲ Savannah Bee Company 📍 Mon-Sat: 10 AM-7 PM | **Sun: 11 AM-6 PM**

💲 $8 to $50 is the average price range.

ITEMS TO PURCHASE

The smooth, buttery flavor of Tupelo honey makes it one of the rarest and most valuable honeys in the United States.

Honey-Infused Body Products: Natural body butters, lotions, and lip balms made with honey from the area.

Local Meads: Sample their sweet and dry honey wine varieties.

Pro Tip: 🍯 Don't miss the complimentary honey tasting bar, where you can try unique blends like Black Sage and Acacia.

Savannah, GA 31406 🌳 Byrd Cookie Company 📍 6700 Waters Ave 🔔 Sun: 12 PM to 5 PM | Mon-Sat: 9 AM to 6 PM $ The typical price range is $7 to $25.

- **Items to Purchase:**

Important Lime Coolers: tart, sweet, and sprinkled with powdered sugar.

Cheddar Pecan Biscuits - A savory Southern snack ideal with wine or drinks.

Gift Tins - Beautifully packed cookies and biscuits, excellent for gifting.

Pro Tip: ⚫ Grab free samples at the counter—it's hard to leave without a bag or two!

The Savannah Soap Company 📍 314 W Broughton St, Savannah, GA 31401 🔔 Mon–Sat: 10 AM – 6 PM | Sun: 12 PM – 5 PM 💲 Average Price Range: $6 – $30

- **Items to Purchase:**

Handcrafted Soaps — Made with natural oils and botanicals, in flavors like Georgia Peach and Magnolia Blossom.

1• **Bath Bombs & Scrubs** – Relaxing lavender bath bombs and exfoliating sugar scrubs.

2• **Gift Sets** — Beautifully wrapped soap sets, perfect for gifting.

📌 **Pro Tip:** 🧼 Their mild and nourishing goat milk soap is a favorite among those with sensitive skin.

Where to Stay - Accommodations for Every Traveler

8.1. Historic Inns and Charming Bed & Breakfasts

Savannah's wide variety of lodging options demonstrates its warmth and friendliness. Savannah offers a variety of lodging options, including historic bed & breakfasts, luxurious boutique hotels with first-rate amenities, and affordable lodgings without sacrificing charm. This is your comprehensive guide to the top lodging options, catered to all kinds of tourists.

Savannah's historic inns and bed and breakfasts provide tasteful rooms, individualized service, and a genuine flavor of Southern hospitality for a visit that transports you back in time.

Savannah, GA 31401

🔔 The Gastonian

📍 220 E Gaston St   Check-out time: 11 AM | Check-in time: 3 PM

💲 Prices start at $250 per night.

- **Reasons to Remain:**

The Gastonian, located in two adjacent 19th-century houses and within a short distance from Forsyth Park, is frequently named one of Savannah's best bed and breakfasts. It has a charming, rustic charm with clawfoot tubs, fireplaces, and antique furniture.

- **Benefits:**

Free breakfast is provided in the garden or in the room.

Every day, there is wine and hors d'oeuvres in the afternoon, followed by sweets and drinks in the evening.

Pro Tip: 🌿 For the utmost seclusion, choose the Carriage House apartment, which is well-liked for anniversaries and honeymoons.

330 Abercorn St., Savannah, GA 31401, Hamilton-Turner Inn

Check-out time: 11 AM | Check-in time: 3 PM 💲 Prices start at $270 per night.

Why Stay: With chandeliers, stately staircases, and cozy chambers, this exquisite Victorian estate on Lafayette Square—which was featured in Midnight in the Garden of Good and Evil—offers a sumptuous stay.

- **Benefits:**

A wonderful breakfast in the South

Wine and cheese in the afternoon

Cookies and port in the evening

📌 **Pro Tip:** According to rumors, the inn is haunted, making it the ideal choice for adventurers seeking a creepy Savannah experience.

14 W Hull St, Savannah, GA 31401 🏠 Foley House Inn 🐾 Check-out time: 11 AM | Check-in time: 3 PM 💲 Prices start at $200 per night.

Why Stay: Offering a fusion of European flair and Southern charm, this little B&B has a view of Chippewa Square. It's perfect for a comfortable, private stay, with 19 distinctively themed rooms and a lovely private garden.

- **Benefits:**

Free gourmet breakfast

Tea and cakes in the afternoon

Hors d'oeuvres and wine in the evening

📌 **Pro Tip:** 🍷 In the evening, sip wine in the garden courtyard—it's a tranquil respite from the busy city.

8.2 Exquisite Hotels & Boutique Accommodations

Savannah's luxury hotels and boutique properties offer the ultimate upmarket experience if you're searching for upscale facilities, exquisite décor, and first-rate service.

⭐ **A Luxury Collection Hotel**, The Perry Lane Hotel 📍 256 E Perry St, Savannah, GA 31401 🔔 Check-out time: 11 AM | Check-in time: 4 PM 💲 Starting rates are $350 per night.

Why Stay: The Perry Lane Hotel offers chic accommodations, carefully chosen artwork, and faultless service while fusing Southern charm with contemporary elegance. Peregrin, its rooftop bar, has some of Savannah's best views.

Benefits:
Rooftop lounge and pool
The Emporium Kitchen & Wine Market offers excellent on-site eating.
Free bicycles to use for city exploration

📌 **Pro Tip:** 🍸 Peregrin's rooftop cocktails are a must-try, especially after sunset for expansive views.

400 W River St, Savannah, GA 31401 ⭐ JW Marriott Savannah Plant Riverside District 📍 🔔 Check-out time: 11 AM | Check-in time: 4 PM 💲 Starting rates are $400 per night.

- **Reasons to Remain:**

This JW Marriott combines elegance and industrial architecture in a repurposed power station on River Street. Live music, food, and shopping can all be found in the Plant Riverside District.

Benefits:
Live music and views of the river
On-site galleries and a gemstone museum
Numerous eateries and bars, including the rooftop Moon Skytop Lounge Pro Electric Advice: 🌙 Ask for a room with a view of the river so you can observe the cargo ships passing by.

412 Williamson St., Savannah, GA 31401 🔔 The Alida, Savannah Check-out time: 11 AM | Check-in time: 4 PM 💲 Prices start at $320 per night.

Why Stay: The Alida, which is conveniently located near River Street, combines contemporary elegance with old world charm. It's ideal for kids and couples alike because of its warm atmosphere, artisan touches, and rooftop bar.

Benefits:
The Lost Square, a rooftop bar with expansive river views
A pool of saltwater with cabanas
Southern cuisine served on-site at The Rhett Pro
• **Advice**: 🥂 Savor sunset cocktails at The Lost Square, a popular spot for both locals and tourists.

💰 8.3 Affordable Choices and Comfortable Rentals

Savannah provides plenty of cheap hotels that nonetheless pack in charm and comfort. Here are the greatest budget-friendly lodgings without losing the Savannah experience.

611 W Oglethorpe Ave, Savannah, GA 31401 🐸
The Thunderbird Inn 💡 Check-out time: 11 AM | Check-in time: 3 PM 💲 Starting rates are $130 per night.
Why Stay: With mid-century contemporary furnishings and quirky extras like free MoonPies

and RC Cola in your room, this retro-chic motel has a fun and quirky attitude.

> **Benefits:**

Free coffee and Krispy Kreme doughnuts every morning
- Pet-friendly accommodations
- The Historic District is within walking distance.

📌 **Pro Tip:** ● Before you go exploring, have a free doughnut and coffee from the lobby.

123 E Broughton St, Savannah, GA 31401
🔔 The Marshall House
📍 Check-out time: 11 AM | Check-in time: 4 PM
$ Starting rates are $180 per night.

- **Reasons to Remain:**

The Marshall House, which was constructed in 1851 and features antique furnishings, exposed brick walls, and a hint of haunted history, offers reasonably priced luxury.

- **Benefits:**

Free reception with wine and cheese
Free continental breakfast

📌 **Pro Tip:** 👻 Ideally situated on busy Broughton Street Inquire about ghost stories at the hotel—

The Marshall House is regarded as one of the most eerie hotels in Savannah.

Comfortable Airbnb & Rental Choices

Prices range from $90 to $150 per night.
There are several Airbnb and VRBO options in Savannah's quaint districts, ranging from contemporary lofts to antique carriage houses. Ideal for families who seek additional space or for longer stays.

➤ Top Rental Neighborhoods:
1• Historic District: All of the main sites are accessible on foot
2• Starland District: A trendy neighborhood with fashionable cafés and art galleries
3• Victorian District: lovely old houses with peaceful, tree-lined streets

📌 **Pro Tip:** 🔑 Seek out apartments with balconies or private courtyards, which are ideal for enjoying morning coffee while surrounded by Spanish moss.

Useful Advice for a Stress-Free Journey

✔ Walking, Biking, and Trolleys in Savannah

With its historic layout, Savannah is a pedestrian-friendly city that is simple to explore on foot. However, the city has a range of modes of transportation, like as ferries, bike rentals, and trolley excursions, for those seeking a more laid-back way to get around. Here's how to make traveling about Savannah easy and fun, whether your preference is to stroll along the Savannah River, take a trolley tour, or wander beneath the oak-lined streets.

- **Walking**: Walking is the best way to explore Savannah's Historic District. One of the most walkable cities in the United States, the small 2.5-square-mile area boasts 22 historic squares, broad walkways, and shaded streets.

  ➢ **Why Take a Walk?**

  ✔ **Simple Navigation:** Most shops, eateries, and sights are within ten to fifteen minutes' walk from one another.

  ✔ **Beautiful Streets:** The cobblestone walkways, trees covered with Spanish moss, and old buildings provide a lovely walk.

  ✔ **Cost-effective:** You can explore at your own speed and walk for free.

The best places to walk are from Forsyth Park to River Street, which is a relaxing 30-minute stroll through the squares that ends at the busy riverfront. Bull Street Corridor: Take a stroll past the Savannah Theatre and Chippewa Square

(Forrest Gump Square) from Forsyth Park to City Market.

● Walk by the Davenport House Museum, Owens-Thomas House & Slave Quarters, and Mercer-Williams House as part of the Historic Homes Tour.

✦ **Tip:** River Street and certain historic districts feature uneven cobblestones that might be difficult to walk on, so wear comfortable shoes.

Trolley Tours: A Calm and Educational Experience

Trolley tours in Savannah offer a picturesque, escorted experience that lets you see the city without becoming overly exhausted. Because these excursions are hop-on, hop-off, you can pause at sights and resume your journey at a later time.

Top Trolley Companies

1 **Old Town Trolley Tours**

📍 Several stops in the Historic District

💰 **Cost**: $20.84 for children (ages 4-12) | $41.68 for adults

📍 The route includes 15 stations, such as River Street, City Market, and Forsyth Park. 🎫 Tickets: Purchase online to save money; admittance on the second day is free.

2 **Old Savannah Tours' Savannah Hop-On Hop-Off Trolley**

📍 Several stops across the city

💰 **Cost**: $39 for adults and $20 for children

Route: 16 stops, with period-appropriate live guides who make history interesting and entertaining.

🎫 **Bonus: Most hotels offer free shuttle service.**

🚌 **Ideal for:** First-time tourists seeking a leisurely, instructive experience while taking in the main attractions.

- **Advice**: To avoid lengthy walks between important attractions if you're pressed for time, take the hop-on, hop-off option.

Biking: An Exciting and Beautiful Choice
Because of Savannah's level streets, bicycling is a fun and effective method to move around, covering more territory than walking while also taking in the beauty of the city.

Top Rental Bike Stores 🚲 Savannah On Wheels Standard bikes cost $25 per day, while e-bikes cost $60.

🚲 Perry Rubber Bike Shop: Hourly and daily rentals are available.

The Best Bike-Friendly Paths

⬤ The Forsyth Park & Historic District Loop is a picturesque drive past quaint squares, old homes, and lanes lined with trees. Enjoy stunning views of the Savannah River from the Hutchinson Island

Riverwalk, which offers convenient boat connection back to River Street. ● Tybee Island: Only 20 minutes away by vehicle, rent a bike and visit the nearest beach town to Savannah.

■ **Ideal for:** Tourists that prefer to explore the outdoors and seek a quicker alternative to walking to see the city.

♦ **Advice:** Exercise caution when riding close to trolley tracks because it can be challenging to cross them on a bike.

⌂ Ferries, buses, and ridesharing

The majority of transportation needs are met by walking, bicycling, and trams, however for those who need a fast ride or are going outside the Historic District, there are other options.

⌂ Lyft and Uber

✔ Easily accessible all across Savannah.

✔ Be prepared for lengthier wait times during the busiest travel seasons and in the evenings.

✔ It costs about $25 to $35 to take a ride from the Historic District to Tybee Island.

The buses operated by Chatham Area Transit (CAT)

✔ Reasonably priced: $1.50 each ride, with day passes offered.

✔ Routes go through midtown, downtown Savannah, and a few surrounding districts.

✔ The Historic District is served by the free DOT Express Shuttle.

♻ Savannah Belles Ferry

📍 Links Hutchinson Island and River Street

Every 20 to 30 minutes, there is a free ferry service that is ideal for taking in stunning views of the Savannah River without having to deal with traffic. It operates every day from 7 AM to midnight on Monday through Saturday and from 7 AM to 10 PM on Sunday.

■ **Ideal for:** A beautiful, cost-free route between Hutchinson Island and River Street.

9.2 Local Customs, Etiquette, and Safety

Savannah safety

Although Savannah is among the safest places to visit in the United States, as with any city, care should be given, particularly at night.

Places to Stay Away from at Night

Even while much of downtown Savannah is safe, it's advised to stay away from specific places after dark, especially if you're walking alone.

✔ **Secure at Night:**

Historic District (Remain on busy, well-lit streets)

River Street (bustling and bustling, but watch out for your possessions)

Forsyth Park is a popular spot for strolls in the evening, but stay away from the southern end after dark.

🚫 **Use caution when:**

Secluded regions south of Forsyth Park (**low lighting, less foot traffic**) West Savannah, next to I-16 (few activities, not a tourist area)

Eastside communities outside the Historic District

General Safety Advice

- At night, stay in crowded, well-lit locations.
- Keep valuables safe—pickpocketing can happen, especially on River Street during busy hours.
- Avoid flashing cash or expensive things when strolling through crowded places.
- Stay on streets with restaurants, stores, and pedestrian activity.
- Instead of going out alone late at night, use ridesharing applications like Uber or Lyft.
- If you are driving, avoid leaving items in your car that are visible, especially in parking garages or on River Street.

- **Advice:** Enter a restaurant, store, or hotel lobby if you ever feel lost or uneasy; locals and business owners are typically pleased to help guests.

◆ **Regional Customs & Etiquette**

Savannah's laid-back vibe and amiable residents are what make it so charming. Observe these basic etiquette guidelines to fit in and take full use of the city.

1. Saluting Residents

✔ **Say Hello:** Even when interacting with strangers, it's customary to say "Good morning" or "How are you?"

✔ **Anticipate Small Talk**: People in Savannah are friendly and gregarious, so it's normal for store owners, bartenders, or even complete strangers to start a discussion.

✔ **Be Polite:** Saying "Thank you, ma'am/sir," when someone holds the door open for you, is always appreciated.

2. Clothes Code

Savannah enjoys traditional Southern charm despite its laid-back attitude.

✔ **Casual Clothing**: Appropriate for most locations, such as cafes, casual dining establishments, and daytime sightseeing.

✔ **Business Casual**: Necessary in upmarket hotels, cocktail lounges, and fine dining establishments.

✔ **Churches & Historic Sites**: When visiting places of worship, stay away from clothing that is too exposing or beachy.

 ◆ **Advice**: Wear a lovely dress, button-down shirt, or chic ensemble if you're dining at a fancy restaurant like The Grey or The Olde Pink House.

3. Laws Concerning Open Containers

One of the few places in the United States where open alcohol containers are permitted is Savannah.

 As long as they are in plastic to-go cups, you are allowed to carry alcoholic beverages throughout the Historic District.

✔ **It is not possible**: Keep all beverages in plastic cups; don't bring glass bottles or cans.

Enter bars and restaurants with alcohol from outside. Outside of the Historic District, carry open beverages (the law does not apply outside of downtown).

* **Advice**: You can enjoy your drink while walking through the squares because many bars provide "to-go" beverages.

4. The Culture of Tipping

In Savannah, tipping is customary in the majority of service sectors.

* **The Normal Tipping Guide:**

20% for good service and 25% for great service at restaurants and bars.

Ghost tour guides and trolley tours cost $5 to $10 per participant, depending on the length of the tour.

Housekeeping at the hotel: $3 to $5 each night.

Bartenders: 20% of the entire cost or $1 to $2 each drink.

$5 to $10 for valet parking when you pick up your vehicle.

◆ **Tips**: Service personnel frequently depend on gratuities, and Savannah is a city that relies on visitors. Don't be reluctant to leave a generous tip if you receive excellent service.

9.3 Example Routes: Two-, three-, and week-long excursions

■ Savannah Itinerary for Two Days (Weekend Retreat)

Day 1: Culture & History

☀ **Good morning:**

Explore Forsyth Park and stop by the fountain to snap pictures.

Discover the Midnight in the Garden of Good and Evil at Mercer-Williams House.

🌙 **Evening and afternoon:**

Southern comfort food is served for lunch in Mrs. Wilkes' dining room.

Explore the art galleries and shops in City Market.

Nighttime Haunted Ghost Tour.

🖼️ Savannah Itinerary for Three Days (Long Weekend)

Day 1: The same as the two-day schedule.

Day 2: Riverfront & Outdoor

☀ Good morning:

Examine the Bonaventure Cemetery.

Explore the Historic District on a bicycle or trolley trip.

🌙 Evening and afternoon:

Vic's on the River (a waterfront restaurant) for lunch.

Take the Savannah Belles Ferry and stroll along River Street.

Peregrin Rooftop Bar drinks.

Savannah Itinerary for Three Days (Long Weekend)

Day 1: The same as the two-day schedule.

Day 2: Riverfront & Outdoor ☀ Good morning:

Examine the Bonaventure Cemetery.

Explore the Historic District on a bicycle or trolley trip.

🌙 Evening and afternoon:

Vic's on the River (a waterfront restaurant) for lunch.

Take the Savannah Belles Ferry and stroll along River Street.

- **Peregrin Rooftop Bar drinks.**

The itinerary for a week in Savannah includes the following activities:

Day 1: Historic District & Museums;

Day 2: River Street & City Market;

Day 3: Bonaventure Cemetery & Tybee Island;

Day 4: Ghost Tours & Nightlife;

Day 5: Shopping & Local Markets;

Day 6: Art & Culture; and

Day 7: Relaxation & Spa Day.

➢ **INSTRUCTIONS**

1• Kindly Ensure You Open The Video Travel Log Appropriately.

2• Download Snaptube Apk, install on your Device Then Open The QR code with it.

3• Scan the Qr code and Open with Snaptube, ensure You have internet Access.

FINAL THOUGHTS

1• Maximizing Your Visit to Savannah

Savannah is a city best experienced slowly because of its walkability, historic charm, and welcoming environment. There are many undiscovered treasures in this city, whether you're exploring haunting legends, enjoying a cocktail on River Street, or taking a leisurely stroll around Forsyth Park.

📌 **Pro Tips for a Stress-Free Trip:**

■ Make reservations in advance because spring and fall are the busiest times of year.

■ Get up early to beat the crowds and humidity.

■ For a convenient, escorted experience, use the trolley excursions.

■ Remember to pack a reusable water bottle because the warm Savannah weather can cause dehydration.

You will want more from Savannah's history, cuisine, and Southern charm no matter how long you stay!

" DEAR READER IF YOU REALLY ENJOYED THIS GUIDE KINDLY LEAVE AN HONEST REVIEW ON THE PRODUCT PAGE OF THIS BOOK ON AMAZON".

Made in the USA
Middletown, DE
17 April 2025

74413361R00089